THIS BOOK BELONGS TO:

_____

_____

_____

mantra

For the children of Richard Cobden Primary School, London
D.M.

Special thanks to Phillip Fong and his family,
and to the staff and children of Mason Avenue Kindergarten
J.C.

First published 2003 by Mantra
5 Alexandra Grove, London N12 8NU
www.mantralingua.com

British Library Cataloguing in Publication Data:
a catalogue record for this book is available
from the British Library.

Il Dente Traballante

The Wibbly Wobbly Tooth

Written by David Mills
Illustrated by Julia Crouth

Italian translation by Paola Antonioni

mantra

Lunedi sera, due minuti dopo le sette: in quel momento il dente di Lì dondolò per la prima volta.
E il dente fece clic clac.

On Monday evening at two minutes past seven, Li got his first wobbly tooth.
And the tooth went...Wibble Wobble.

Martedì lo fece vedere a tutti i bambini a scuola.
E il dente fece clic clac.

On Tuesday, he had to show everyone at school.
And the tooth went...Wibble Wobble.

Mercoledì dovette fare attenzione mentre mangiava, a mezzogiorno.
E il dente fece clic clac, clic clac.

On Wednesday, he had to be careful eating his lunch.
And the tooth went...Wibble, Wobble, Wibble, Wobble.

Giovedì Lì dovette fare molta attenzione nel lavarsi i denti.
E il dente fece clic clac, clic clac, clic clac.

On Thursday, Li had to be extremely careful brushing his teeth.
And the tooth went...Wibble, Wobble, Wibble Wobble Wibble.

Venerdì il suo dente girava
dentro e fuori…

On Friday, Li wiggled his tooth in
and out,

Lo girò e lo mise persino sotto la lingua
finché fece…

he twisted it and even stuck his tongue under it,
until it went...

CLIC CLAC, CLIC CLAC,
CLIC CLAC…
OOPS!

WIBBLE WOBBLE, WIBBLE
WOBBLE.
WIBBLE WOBBLE…
OOOOPS!

"HURRAY!" everyone cheered.
Li gave them a big smile and he felt very brave.

"Urrà!!" Gridarono tutti.
Lì sorrise e si sentì molto coraggioso.

Quando fu ora di andare a casa, Lì corse fuori per farsi
vedere dal suo papà.

When it was time to go home, Li rushed out to show his dad.

"Finalmente!" disse il papà,
"Bravo!"

"At last," said Dad.
"Well done!"

Sabato a Lì mancava il suo dentino anteriore.
Avrebbe tanto voluto un dente nuovo.

On Saturday, Li missed his front tooth.
He really wanted a new tooth.

"Vieni," disse il papà, "andiamo a trovare la nonna. Lei saprà cosa fare."
E cosi andarono dalla nonna…

"Come on," said Dad, "let's go and see Grandma. She'll know just what to do."
So off they went to Grandma's.

"Guarda!" disse Lì.
"Ehi, hai perso un dente!" disse Joey. "Se lo metti sotto il cuscino,
la fata dei denti arriverà e ti porterà dei soldi!"
"Perché?" chiese Lì.
"Le serve il tuo dente per costruirsi una casa nuova!"
"Oh," disse Lì. "Devo dirlo alla nonna!"

"Look!" said Li.
"Hey, you've lost your tooth!" said Joey.
"If you put it under the pillow, the tooth
fairy will come and bring you some money!"
"Why?" asked Li.
"She needs your tooth to build
her new house!"
"Oh," said Li. "I'd better tell
my Grandma!"

"Guarda!" disse Lì.
"Ooooooh!" disse Kofi. "Io ho nascosto il mio nella terra,
e me ne è arrivato uno nuovo!"
"Davvero? Devo dirlo alla nonna!"

"Look!" said Li.
"Oooooo!" said Kofi. "I hid mine
in the ground and then my new
one grew!"
"Did it really? I must tell my
Grandma!"

"Guarda!" disse Lì.
"Ehi," disse Salma. "Potresti gettare il tuo dente nel fiume!
Ti porterà buona fortuna!"
"Davvero?" disse Lì. "Papà, cosa devo fare?"
"La nonna lo sa," disse il papà.

"Look!" said Li.
"Hey," said Salma. "You could throw your
tooth into the river and it will
bring you good luck!"
"It will?" said Li. "Dad, what shall
I do?"
"Grandma knows," said Dad.

"Nonna, nonna, GUARDA!!" Disse Lì, "Il mio dente ha fatto CLIC CLAC, CLIC CLAC, CLIC CLAC e FUORI!"
"Bene, bene, bene," sorrise la nonna. "Io so precisamente cosa fare! Buttalo sopra il tetto di un vicino ed esprimi un desiderio," sussurrò.
"OK," gridò Lì e…

"Grandma, grandma, LOOK!" said Li. "My tooth went WIBBLE WOBBLE WIBBLE WOBBLE WIBBLE WOBBLE and OUT!"
"Well, well, well," smiled Grandma. "I know just what to do!" she whispered. "Throw it up onto a neighbour's roof and make a big wish."
"OK," shouted Li and...

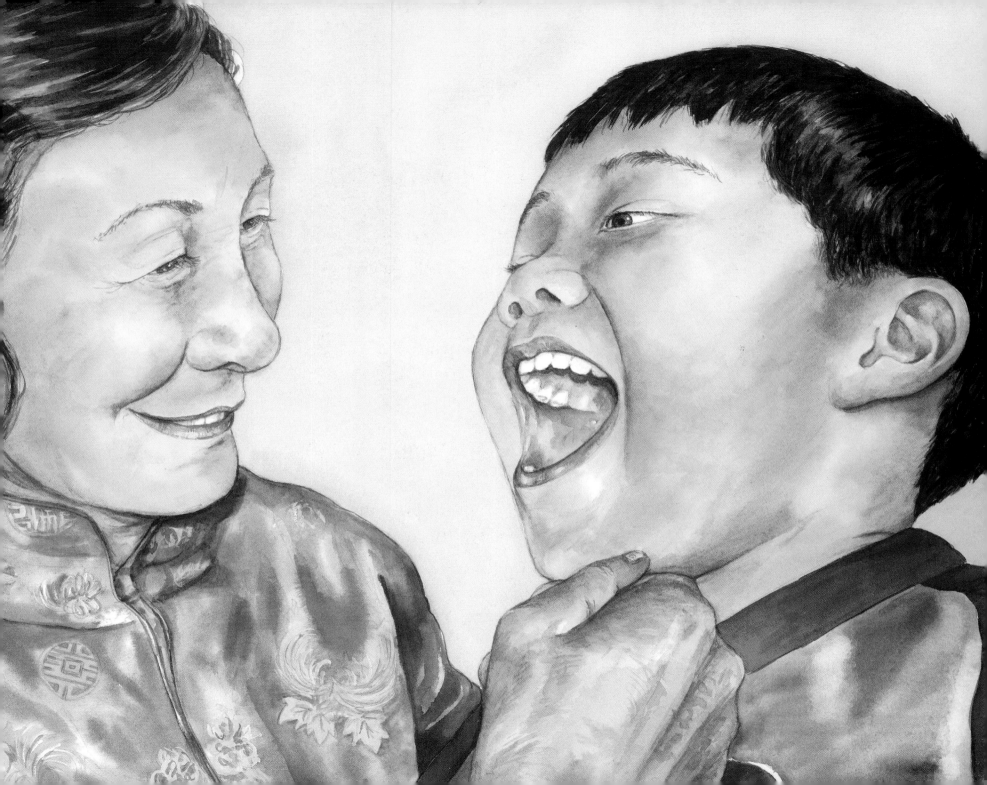

...buttò il suo dente in aria con tutta la sua forza!

...threw his tooth up with all his might!

Il giorno successivo era domenica.
E non successe niente.

The next day was Sunday
and nothing happened.

Ma la domenica seguente, due minuti dopo le sette,
il desiderio di Lì si realizzò!

But the next Sunday morning at two minutes past seven, Li's wish came true!

"Mamma, papà" sussurrò Lì "guardate!"

"Mum, Dad," whispered Li. "Look!"

TOOTHY QUESTIONS

1. Have you lost your first tooth yet?

2. What do we need our teeth for?

3. How do you take care of your teeth?

4. When did you last visit the dentist?

5. Which one of these is best for taking care of teeth?
   a. Eating chocolate
   b. Brushing your teeth twice a day
   c. Climbing a tree

6. In some parts of the world people use different things to clean their teeth. Can you guess which they use?
   a. Apples
   b. Tea leaves
   c. Twigs

7. Which of these animals have the biggest teeth?
   a. Rats
   b. Wolves
   c. Elephants

TOOTHY ANSWERS

2. We need our teeth for eating and talking. They also make us look good when we smile!

5. Brushing your teeth twice a day.

6. Twigs from the Neem tree which grows in South Asia. They fight bacteria, protecting both the teeth and gums. The Neem tree is well known for its medicinal uses.

7. Elephants. Did you know that the tusks of an African elephant can grow up to 3.5 meters!